Original title:
The Ocean's Whisper

Copyright © 2025 Creative Arts Management OÜ
All rights reserved.

Author: Nolan Kingsley
ISBN HARDBACK: 978-1-80581-676-8
ISBN PAPERBACK: 978-1-80581-203-6
ISBN EBOOK: 978-1-80581-676-8

Dances on the Dunes

Seagulls laugh at the sandy sway,
Crabs are doing their crabby ballet.
Waves play tag with feet and toes,
Shells giggle as the cold wind blows.

Flip-flops fly through the salty air,
Sunburned noses, not a single care.
A sunbather snores in a sandy heap,
While someone's cooler goes splish and leap.

Glistening Horizons

Fish wearing glasses swim in a row,
Chasing after the sun's golden glow.
Octopus juggles shells with a grin,
While turtles race, determined to win.

A beach ball bounces, oh what a sight,
As kids chase it, with pure delight.
The horizon winks like it knows a jest,
While the tide plays hide and seek with the rest.

Nightfall's Serenity

Stars throw parties on the dark blue sea,
Moonlight shines, just like glittery confetti.
Crickets chirp with a comedic beat,
While dolphins dance as they skip and greet.

Ghost crabs waltz under the moon's glow,
Practicing steps in a dim, soft-flow.
The night whispers jokes to the gentle tide,
As the sun snores loud, enjoying the ride.

Composed by the Deep

Turtles play chess in a kelp-filled hall,
Sounds of laughter echo, oh what a ball!
Fish orchestra tunes in the bright coral,
A symphony of bubbles, how truly floral.

Whales wear tuxedos, ready to perform,
Laughing at seals who don't fit the norm.
Jellyfish glow as they sway like a dance,
In the depths where the silly take their chance.

Whispers of Ancient Mariner

In salty air, where seagulls screech,
A captain dances on the beach.
His tales of fish are far from true,
They might just be from last week's stew.

He swears he caught a whale so grand,
But really, it was just a band.
Of jellyfish that danced in a line,
And stole his dinner, oh so fine!

With tales of storms and ships that sink,
He laughs and spills his rum to drink.
But all the fish just roll their eyes,
For with his tales, the truth just dies.

So here's to all the fishy yarns,
That wobble as they walk the barns.
The ancient mariner's got some clout,
But don't you dare believe his shout.

Beneath the Moonlight's Glow

Under the stars, where crabs parade,
The moon looks down, a silver blade.
A fish named Larry sings a tune,
While mermaids giggle at the moon.

"Oh, come and dance!" the sea-nymphs call,
While sailors trip and tumble, fall.
The waves just chuckle, roll away,
As fish throw shells in a playful fray.

The moonlit waves hide many pranks,
Like cheeky shrimp in pirate tanks.
They laugh and splash, oh what a sight,
As sailors wish they'd stayed on land for the night.

So let's raise a toast with seaweed stew,
To all the laughs that bubbles brew.
As stars wink down on all the cheer,
The ocean's giggles serve us here.

The Call of Siren's Song

In watery depths, a voice does tease,
With notes that swirl and ebb like breeze.
"Come hither, sailors, join our fun!"
But all they find is seaweed bun.

Oh, sirens sing of gold and glee,
But they just want your lunch, you see.
With shiny shells and tasty bait,
They beckon you—it's surely fate!

One sailor brave, named Timmy Boo,
Dived in to grab a fish or two.
But all he found was a shoe instead,
And then he left, with tales of dread.

So mark my words, do heed this cheer,
Don't trust the songs that you might hear.
For in the deep where mermaids sway,
It's just a ruse for a fish buffet!

Secrets in the Coral

In coral caves, where secrets crawl,
The fish all giggle, having a ball.
They swap their tales of lives so grand,
While crabs just pinch and take a stand.

A clownfish jokes, "I'm here to play!
Just don't confuse me with my heyday."
He tells of times he wore a hat,
And danced with octopuses—imagine that!

The sea turtle shakes his ancient head,
"I've seen more than you in my bed!
I've napped with dolphins, it's all a dream,
But bubbles rise and fishy schemes."

So gather round near coral's edge,
For laughter calls and jokes will hedge.
The secrets here are fun and bright,
In this underwater party night!

Celestial Reflections

Under the moon, fish dance around,
With jellybeans floating, they make no sound.
A crab wears a hat, oh what a sight,
As seagulls below dive for fish in flight.

Stars twinkle above in a wobbly way,
Larry the lobster wants to join the ballet.
He slips on a shell, lands right in the sea,
All laughing out loud, oh what a spree!

Distant Shores Calling

On sandy dunes, we build castles bright,
Only to watch as the waves take a bite.
The tide giggles softly, 'You call that a moor?'
As sandcastles crumble, we roll on the floor.

Turtles in sunglasses slide by in style,
They wink at our mess, then strike a cool smile.
As the sun sets low, we dance with delight,
With piña coladas that taste just right!

Waves of Memory

Seashells tell tales, it's true they do speak,
Of pirates and treasure, of paths we must seek.
But our dog steals the snacks, oh what a thief!
He digs up the past, yes, quite beyond belief!

The gulls squawk in laughter, it's quite a show,
As we chase our lost chips, all fast and slow.
But ocean delights, like a carefree breeze,
Bring joy and sweet chuckles, oh yes, if you please!

Embrace of the Sea Breeze

Dancing with kites, we float in the air,
The wind flips our hats, oh do beware!
A seagull pecks gently, it thinks we're a snack,
As we run in circles, 'Hey! Get off my back!'

Tide pools are giggling, where crabs play roles,
In a clam's theater, with madcap goals.
The waves give a chuckle, their foamy delight,
As we splash and we tumble, 'til day turns to night.

Mystical Marine Melodies

Bubbles dance, fish wear hats,
Octopus jokes, and playful chats.
Seaweed sways like a groovy band,
While crabs do a silly happy stand.

Starfish giggle on the warm sand,
Their laughter, a wave from a magical land.
Seagulls squawk with comic flair,
As dolphins dive without a care.

Jellyfish float with a jiggy sway,
Chasing sunbeams throughout the day.
Mermaids sing with ridiculous tones,
Brushing their hair made of seashells and bones.

Shells and Stories

A clam tells tales of a lost shoe,
While snails compete in a slow-view zoo.
Crabs boast of treasure, so shiny, so bright,
But it's just an old bottle, oh what a sight!

Seashells gather, swapping their lore,
About surfers who fell and rolled on the shore.
Starfish recite their rhythmic plays,
While sea cucumbers nap through the day.

With each wave, laughter spills wide,
As fish in tuxedos take a ride.
Shrimps laugh hard at their funny fate,
Wearing tiny top hats, oh isn't it great?

Silent Waters Speak

The sea chuckles softly, a hidden muse,
With crabs wearing glasses, they can't refuse.
A whale hums jokes through a mighty spray,
While sardines form a conga line play.

Turtles shuffle, with style and grace,
And shrimp do the cha-cha in a race.
The buoys bob like they're in a dance,
As mermaids giggle, caught in a trance.

The tide teases with a playful splash,
Shells hear whispers of a silly bash.
Every ripple holds a funny tale,
Under the warmth of the sunlit veil.

The Call of the Tide

Wave after wave, they dance and glide,
Seagulls dive in, with a splashy slide.
The fish are giggling, they play hide and seek,
Getting tickled by bubbles, they all squeak!

Crabs in their shells do the moonwalk,
Chasing each other like they're in a rock.
The jellybeans jiggle, with laughter afloat,
While octopuses join in, wearing a coat!

Mermaid's Lament

A mermaid was singing, but slipped on a clam,
"Why do I wear pearls? I'm more of a jam!"
Her scales sparkled bright, but she tripped on a wave,
"I'll only swim slow, if I can misbehave!"

With dolphins around, she blew bubbles of glee,
"Why swim in circles, when you can chase me?"
Her hair tangled up, like a kelp salad bowl,
"Underwater chaos, that's how I roll!"

Secrets of the Salty Depths

Whispers and giggles, beneath the deep blue,
Where squids tell secrets and fish toast a brew.
The rocks all chuckle at the feisty tide,
While merlings play games, with no place to hide.

"Did you hear the clam snore?" said an old sea star,
"Or how the sea turtle dances with a guitar?"
Jellyfish float by, giving everyone hugs,
As sea cucumbers rock out in their rugs!

Sighs of the Surf

The waves send whispers, calling out loud,
"Join us, dear beach, you should be proud!"
Sandcastles tumble at the beachcomber's feet,
While sand crabs perform their silly retreat.

Seashells clink together, a catchy tune,
As kids in their buckets dance under the moon.
"Let's build a big fortress, then watch it all fall!"
The laughter erupts and echoes through all!

Ocean's Heartbeat

The waves wear a cheeky grin,
As they play hide and seek with the sun,
Seagulls gossip, too loud to ignore,
While fish wear sunglasses, just for fun.

Crabs throw a party on the soft sand,
They dance in their little sideways way,
Shells are the VIPs, all decked out,
Bouncing around—what a wild display!

A dolphin jokes, flips with great flair,
'Why did the fish cross the road, you see?
To get to the other tide, oh so rare!'
The ocean laughs, a bubbly decree.

A mermaid laughs, tickles a whale,
With a tickle fight in the bright blue sea,
Bubbles pop like laughter in the foam,
Who knew nature was so silly and free?

Dance of the Sea Breeze

The wind winks and teases a kite,
It dances like a joyfully mad sprite,
Shells spin around, caught in delight,
As the sea hums a tune, just right.

Sandcastles giggle, tipsy and tall,
As waves sneak in and give them a call,
'Hey, don't drown!' they all seem to stall,
While starfish clap and join in the brawl.

A curious crab dons a beach hat,
Sips seaweed juice, and a critter spat,
"Why so salty?" a clam asks, quite fat,
"Just livin' it up, imagine that!"

Seagulls hold meetings, debating the tides,
With snacks of pizza, oh how it slides,
They squawk about land, where laughter collides,
In this fun dance, where joy never hides.

Embracing the Infinite Blue

The sky bends down, whispers a joke,
While waves snicker, circling like smoke,
A fish wearing a top hat says, 'Folks,
It's time for a swim, don't be so broke!'

A turtle, slow, but spills a big laugh,
'I'm just on a quest for the finest sea staff,'
While dolphins chase bubbles, oh what a gaff,
Creating a splash with each playful half.

Octopuses juggle, quite deft and ace,
Seahorses cheer as they trot in their space,
A crab throws a conch, it lands with grace,
A comedy show, it's a delightful place.

The moon joins in, grinning so wide,
A party of waves in rhythmic glide,
The ocean's spirit won't ever hide,
In this funny dance, we happily abide.

Wandering Waves

Waves roll in, a cheeky surprise,
They tease the shore with mischievous eyes,
'Got your shoes wet, oh what a prize!'
Chasing their laughter, the tide smartly flies.

The starfish all lounge, sipping saltwater tea,
Fish make faces, wild as can be,
With a wink and a flip, they dart, oh wee!
Playing tag with the breeze, free as a spree.

A hermit crab dreams of a mansion so grand,
Eats too much algae, can't quite understand,
'Why is my shell now a beachy band stand?'
In this silly world, everything's unplanned.

As gulls storm in, calling for food,
They squawk about lunch in a raucous mood,
With laughter so loud, it's a joyful brood,
Among wandering waves, where life feels good.

Light Beneath the Surface

A fish in a hat, it danced on a wave,
With sunglasses on, oh how it misbehaved!
Crabs joined a conga, they shimmied with glee,
"Dance like no one's watching!" they shouted with glee.

The jellyfish twirled, oh what a sight,
In sparkly colors, they glimmered so bright.
"Catch me if you can," the seagulls they squawked,
As seaweed confetti danced and then rocked.

A dolphin gave chase, but tripped on a shell,
Spinning and flopping, it flew like a bell.
With laughter and bubbles they splashed all around,
In this underwater circus, joy could be found.

So if you dive deep, take a peek and you'll see,
The antics of critters who swim wild and free.
Beneath all the waves, they party all day,
With giggles and splashes, they frolic and play.

Haikus from the Harbor

Fish with tiny hats,
Balancing on the bow,
Giggles fill the air.

Seagulls caw a tune,
Tap dancing on the rooftops,
It's a sunny show.

Crabs race on the sand,
Pinching toes as they scuttle,
Who will win the prize?

Waves laugh with the breeze,
Jokes whispered through the sea foam,
Silly jokes for me.

Shimmering Sounds of Serenity

A clam sings a song, oh so out of tune,
The starfish just groans under the moon.
With a wink and a smile, they form a band,
As sea cucumbers shake it, oh so grand!

Turtles doing the cha-cha, what a sight!
While barnacles boogie with all of their might.
A fish with a flute plays a jazzy beat,
Echoes of fun float in every heartbeat.

The crabs catch a wave, all groovy and cool,
Building sandcastles, it's their summer school.
They shout, "Let's dig deeper, find treasures, oh my!"
While seashells keep secrets as they flutter by.

A conch joins the choir, belting out a note,
While minnows form lines in their little boat.
With bubbles as confetti, they groove without care,
These oceanic antics, will make you beware!

Coastal Chronicles

At dawn, a crab brags of catches so grand,
While fish fumble photo-op, there's joy in the sand.
A pelican swoops down, with a plan oh so sly,
"Eat your catch, not me!" he lets out a cry.

The jellyfish juggles, with confidence bold,
While clams tell tall tales of treasures in gold.
A dolphin gets dizzy, just spinning around,
In this wacky seaside where laughs can be found.

The tidepool holds secrets, like jokes on a shelf,
"Who's fittest?" they ponder, as critters play elf.
The seaweed just chuckles, wrapped around a rock,
"I'm the wisest of all," it says with a shock.

So gather your pals for this whimsical route,
Where laughter is tossed like sea foam about.
In the capers of coastlines, beneath skies so blue,
The funny tales bubble, just waiting for you!

The Depths of Solitude

In a blue room under the sun,
A fish wore a hat, just for fun.
He danced with a crab, wiggled with glee,
While a seaweed choir sang merrily.

A jellyfish juggled with style and flair,
With no sense of gravity, floating in air.
A clam with a mustache ruled like a king,
Declaring the day as a silly fish fling.

The octopus made shapes with its countless arms,
As seahorses giggled, enchanted by charms.
A sandcastle fell with a comical crash,
While starfish laughed, having the most fun bash.

Yet, sundown lured them back to their home,
With whispers of waves, their evening poem.
In the depths where silence often sits,
They dream of tomorrow, with giggles and wits.

Saltwind Dreams

A seagull flew by with a sandwich in tow,
As squawking companions wanted a show.
They danced on the docks, all awkward and bright,
    Wings flapping wildly, a comedic sight.

In the surf, a crab did the cha-cha,
While snails on a shell played the maraca.
The breeze made them giggle, they skipped on the sand,
    With laughter that echoed from sea to the land.

Clams told tall tales of treasures they found,
While flounders played poker, so wobbly and round.
A dolphin named Louie flashed a big grin,
    "Join me for some fun, let the laughter begin!"

As sunset painted the horizon red,
The jokes of the sea danced inside each head.
With salt on their cheeks, another day done,
    They watched their antics under the sun.

Rippled Stories

With a flip of its tail, a whale told a tale,
Of fish in tuxedos setting sail.
They sipped on plankton, the finest of brew,
While sea turtles giggled and joined in the queue.

Anemone danced in a vibrant display,
While a pufferfish puffed in a comical way.
The coral band played a jazzy refrain,
As a starfish broke out with moves quite insane.

In a bubble of laughter, the clownfish conspired,
While sea cucumbers probably retired.
They added some salt to their watery jest,
With giggles and splashes, they felt truly blessed.

As dusk draped the sea in a silky cocoon,
They settled their tales, sung puppet cartoons.
With waves wrapping up stories of joy and surprise,
The depths held their laughter beneath starlit skies.

Waves of Memory

A crab with a cap danced on the shore,
As waves rolled in like a jokester's roar.
With seashells as shoes, they pranced to the beat,
And flopped like a fish, truly hard to beat.

The sea breeze tickled, as fish wore their best,
With bubbles for champagne, they partied with zest.
An octopus DJ spun tunes from the deep,
While all of them swayed, losing track of sleep.

A conch shell narrated tales grand and funny,
Of underwater treasures and sparkling honey.
A dolphin flipped high, cracking jokes in the air,
With each splash and roll, spreading giggles everywhere.

As twilight approached, with colors so bold,
They sealed their day's capers in memories gold.
From waves filled with laughter to stories that gleam,
The sea held their secrets, like whispers of dreams.

Nautical Nostalgia

In a boat made of old tin,
We sailed where the seagulls spin.
Pirates in flip-flops, oh what a sight,
Juggling crabs from morning 'til night.

Memories caught in a fishnet's twist,
With splashes and laughter, none could resist.
Every wave brought a tickle or two,
Seasick sailors swore they would stew.

Old treasure maps all marked with 'X',
But every marked spot was just for bad hex.
We dug for gold, found old socks instead,
And joked of the legends that filled us with dread.

Echoes of laughter ride the tide's sway,
As gulls cackle stories of bright sunny days.
With each salty breeze, we raise up our cheer,
For laughter and fun are what we hold dear.

Ripples of Reflection

A fish in a bowler hat swam by,
Winking an eye, with a pie in the sky.
Reflections shimmer, so silly and spry,
While jellyfish dance, oh my, oh my.

Cocooned in the waves, a crab cracks a joke,
Waves of laughter from the sea's hearty folk.
In a world where octopi wear bow ties so neat,
Life's just a party, can't take a seat.

Bubble-blowing whales make musical glee,
And dolphins tune in to the jests of the sea.
As kitesurfing sea turtles take flight,
Splashes of giggles set the scene just right.

With each gentle wave, we toss cares aside,
As sea cucumbers join the fun in broad stride.
Life's just a splash, a hop, and a skip,
In the rippling laughter, we eagerly quip.

Mysterious Waters

Down in the depths where the silliness dwells,
A squid in a tutu starts ringing some bells.
Glow-in-the-dark fish join the trend,
And deep-sea creatures become our old friends.

Puffers in tiaras float by with a grin,
While wise old turtles request to join in.
The mysteries buried make everyone laugh,
Like a clam with a dream of a bubble bath!

Bubbles of secrets, with stories untold,
Of mermaids who danced while the sun turned to gold.
And whispers of wonders that sparkle and shine,
Turn work into play, it's a grand old time!

In these waters where silliness rules,
With every wave come laughter's fine jewels.
So dive in the fun, let your worries be free,
For joyful adventures await in the sea.

A Symphony of Seashells

A band of crabs played a conch shell tune,
As starfish tap danced under the moon.
With every snap, crack, and pop,
The shells formed a rhythm that made us all stop.

Clams on the cymbals keep time with a clap,
A flute played by fish made us all snap.
The laughter cascaded like waves on the sand,
As stingrays grooved with their fins all so grand.

A seashell so shiny, it caught all the light,
Became a microphone for the fish to recite.
Jellyfish jive with their graceful parade,
In this symphony of laughter, how memories are made!

So join in the fun, let your spirits soar high,
With shells as your instruments beneath the blue sky.
For life at the shore is a grand melody,
With laughter and music, we're forever carefree.

Echoes of the Abyss

In the deep, where fish do jest,
A crab in a tux, he's quite the best.
He dances and prances, a sight to behold,
While seaweed sings tales, both funny and bold.

A starfish shared jokes with a shy little clam,
They laughed so hard; oh, what a jam!
A dolphin peeked in, shook his big head,
'You two are bananas, go back to bed!'

The bubbles they blew made quite the scene,
With a jiggling squid in a polka-dot bean.
They tossed seafoam pies, what a delight,
Who knew the abyss could be so bright?

With laughter erupting from coral so grand,
The ocean's a circus, each fish takes a stand.
So if you dive down, bring your own cheer,
For down in the depths, it's a rootin'-tootin' sphere!

Salty Serenade

On the shores, where gulls swirl high,
A fish in a bowtie said, 'Oh my!'
He serenaded shells with a croaky tune,
'I'm the best singer under the moon!'

A crab joined in with his claw as a mic,
Fiddling on kelp, oh what a hype!
They entertained fish swimming by the score,
As a clam waved flags, shouting, 'Encore!'

But a wave came crashing, oh what a mess,
The fish got wet in their fancy dress.
They laughed and splashed, what a crazy sight,
Turning a concert into a water fight!

With bubbles and giggles, they swam all around,
As the seaside joined in with a boisterous sound.
So next time you wander, take heed of their cheer,
For a salty serenade awaits you near!

Driftwood Dreams

On a raft made of driftwood, a seagull sat tight,
Dreaming of donuts and pancakes at night.
He puffed out his chest, then he let out a squawk,
While playing a game of 'Pretend I'm a rock!'

A turtle swam over with a wink and a grin,
'Your dreams are as floaty as the sea's own skin!'
The seagull just laughed, doing spins with glee,
'But the snacks are much sweeter when shared by the sea!'

As jellyfish jingled, providing the beat,
The crab brought the snacks—what a tasty treat!
With sea cucumber juice and clam chowder soup,
They partied and danced; what a wiggly troupe!

With driftwood dreams bubbling up from below,
Life's funny on waves, just go with the flow.
So when you build rafts, make sure to bring cheer,
And swim with the flavors that's salty and clear!

Whispers of the Shore

At the break of dawn, the waves brought a cheer,
With crabs in sombreros, they chilled with a beer.
They whispered sweet secrets to passing boats,
'Join us for laughs and to float like our coats!'

A fish tried to tango, but slipped on a shell,
As seagulls just cackled, 'Oh, what the swell!'
They rolled with the tide, forming giggling piles,
Creating a banquet of first-rate fish smiles.

Then came the starfish with jokes that they swore,
Would knock all the clams right out of their core.
The tide pulled them in, laughter soon spread,
Until jellyfish bumped and all wished they were dead!

But up on the beach, where the sand shimmers bright,
The whispers grew louder; a truly fine sight.
So follow the echoes, don't be afraid,
For where laughter rejoices, happiness stays!

Beneath the Surface

Bubbles rise and then they pop,
Fish are dancing, what a hop.
I wear a snorkel, looking dumb,
But down here, there's no need to run.

Jellyfish waltz, they sway with glee,
In a party that's wild and jelly-free.
I slip on seaweed, it's quite a sight,
The reef's a mess, but oh what delight!

Crabs have hats, they strut around,
While clams just sit without a sound.
I try to join, but get a pinch,
These clever crabs just make me flinch.

So here I float, what a scene!
In underwater realms where I'm a queen.
With laughter bubbling all around,
Beneath the waves, fun can be found.

Song of the Sirens

Mermaids sing with voices bright,
But their jokes? Just a fishy fright.
They lure you in with tales so sweet,
Then break for lunch; it's my loss, what a treat!

With scales that glimmer, they twirl and dive,
But their punchlines? Only the fish can survive.
I try to swim to join their fun,
Only to trip and lose my bun!

They giggle as I flounder near,
Sipping seawater; oh dear, oh dear!
To join their song, I must be brave,
But I can't tell a fin from a wave!

So I splash around, a silly sight,
As mermaids laugh in pure delight.
I may be a joke, but at least I try,
Dancing with dreams beneath the sky.

Lost in the Abyss

In the depths where light can't tread,
I wander lost, just like my bread.
A giant squid gives me a wink,
"Lost?" he asks, "Just take a drink!"

Fish play poker on coral decks,
Telling tales of shipwrecked specks.
I join the game, but my luck is dire,
I'm out of chips; they laugh at my fire!

Eels throw darts; it's quite a game,
I slip and slide, forgetting my name.
The dark's alive with jokes so dark,
I giggle with ghosts, what a lark!

So here I float, in the blue abyss,
Making new friends, who'd guess this bliss?
Lost but happy, in this strange dive,
With laughter echoing; I feel alive!

Chasing the Setting Sun

As the sun dips low, I try to swim,
Chasing shadows on the ocean's rim.
I'm splashing surf, beer in my hand,
Hoping to catch the day's last strand.

Dolphins giggle, they surf the waves,
With twirling tricks that everyone raves.
I attempt a jump, just to impress,
But belly flop! Oh, what a mess!

Crabs are dancing a conga line,
While I'm here fumbling with my wine.
The tide pulls back, I slide on a rock,
"Watch your step!" they warn, "You'll face a shock!"

Yet laughter rings as night takes hold,
In waters warm and stories bold.
Chasing the sun, oh what a fun run,
With every splash, a smile begun!

Songs from the Seafoam

A crab sings in a clumsy beat,
With shells that dance beneath its feet.
A seagull laughs, steals a fry,
And then swoops low to say goodbye.

The starfish plays the ukulele,
While dolphins join, acting so fray.
The waves clap hands, it's quite a show,
As sea cucumbers steal the glow.

An octopus tries to juggle fish,
But ends up with a tangled wish.
"You're all invited to my feast!"
But then forgets, and goes to sleep.

So if you hear a giggling tide,
It's just the sea with friends beside.
In salty air where laughter flies,
The sea's a clown beneath the skies.

The Call of the Brine

A clam whispers secrets that are absurd,
To every fish and passing bird.
The waves respond with giddy glee,
As jellyfish float on the wild spree.

A dolphin dons a party hat,
While seahorses dance, and that is that!
With bubbles popping, they take a chance,
Creating magic with a silly dance.

The sun brings smiles, such a sight,
As stingrays glide in sheer delight.
A turtle shouts, "Hey, watch me glide!"
And then he takes a tumble, wide-eyed.

So listen close to the frothy fun,
Where sea critters play under the sun.
With laughter echoing through the brine,
You'll find each wave is simply divine!

Murmurs of the Coast

The sand makes jokes at every crash,
As crabs line up for a quick splash.
A fishy pun floats through the air,
While flounders flop without a care.

Seashells giggle, they form a band,
With seaweed hair, all dressed quite grand.
The tides hum tunes, a playful wave,
As beach balls bob and misbehave.

A pelican tries on a hat too big,
And waddles over with a jolly jig.
"Join the fun," he squawks with glee,
While everyone swims in harmony.

So hear the chuckles from a fish's mouth,
As the shore sings songs of the south.
With every ripple and every sway,
The coast invites you to laugh and play.

Beneath the Coral Veil

Beneath bright reefs, so vivid and fine,
A grouper jokes, "I'm simply divine!"
While clownfish giggle, chasing their tail,
They craft tales of a lost pirate's whale.

A sea turtle lifts his glasses to see,
"Those underwater selfies are quite a spree!"
As angelfish swipe at a blurry shot,
While losing track of what they've got.

The corals chant in a synchronized beat,
As crustaceans tap dance on tiny feet.
With every twist of the current's flow,
The laughter rises, putting on a show.

So come on down to the colorful scene,
Where the ocean's giggles are always keen.
With winks and nudges in the ocean's swell,
Life beneath waves is a story to tell.

Secrets of the Deep

A fish in a tux, so dapper and neat,
Swims to the dance floor, can't wait to compete.
He struts like a star, with flair and with glee,
But trips on a clam—oh, what a sight to see!

A octopus waiter serves drinks with finesse,
Juggling fine pearls while wearing a dress.
The guests all applaud as he takes a bow,
But slippery shells make him slip—oh wow!

A dolphin named Chuck tells the best silly jokes,
While sea turtles laugh, rolling with pokes.
They chuckle and snort, all in a mess,
As a crab cracks a pun—what a comedic fest!

In the end of the night, with laughter abound,
The creatures of depth make a joyful sound.
A party like this, you must ever keep,
For secrets like these are too fun to sleep!

Lullabies of the Sea

A starfish hums softly, twinkling away,
While seaweed sings lullabies ending the day.
A whale's gentle voice echoes out through the bay,
As snoring sea urchins keep troubles at bay.

The jellyfish flutters, glowing at night,
Tickling little fish in a funny delight.
They all giggle and wiggle, floating around,
In waves of soft whispers, hilariously sound!

The crabs gather 'round for a bedtime tale,
Of treasures and pirates that ride on a whale.
They clap their small claws, filled with sheer delight,
As sea otters yawn, in the glow of moonlight.

With dreams of the surf, these creatures will sleep,
While the moon winks down at the ocean so deep.
Laughter and fish, the night they will keep,
In the lullabies sung where the laughter runs steep!

Currents in Conversation

Two fish take a stroll, gabbing away,
One says, "I love when the seashells all sway!"
The other replies with a scoff and a grin,
"But don't you just hate when sea cucumbers spin?"

A puffer fish pops with a grin and a smile,
"I think I've met a crab with a terribly wry style."
While anglerfish nods, lighting up with a laugh,
"Did you hear that joke about the mermaid's mustache?"

Then a dolphin dives in, tails flipping with grace,
"Guys, what's the best way to prank an old bass?"
They giggle and chortle, in bubbly delight,
As bubbles float up, making sparkles in light.

And as the tides shift, their chatter won't cease,
With jokes and tall tales that never find peace.
In currents of laughter, the ocean's their stage,
Creating small ripples that never grow age!

Moonlit Tides

The moon takes a peek at the sea with a grin,
As fish float by wearing spoons on their chin.
A mackerel laughs, "It's a fashion parade!"
While a crab joins the fray with a shell he has laid.

A seagull drops in, trying hard not to gaff,
"Who knew seashells could make you laugh?"
But a snapper spins tales, in his scaled, jolly way,
Of dolphins that disco at the end of the day.

As tides roll and twirl, they dance in delight,
Counting the stars shining bright in the night.
The waves whisper jokes, in a bubbly embrace,
Where laughter erupts, can't keep off the face!

And when the sun rises, they'll rest from their spree,
For tonight they will gather by the wide, rolling sea.
With humor aplenty and laughter that glides,
They'll continue their fun with the moonlit tides!

Currents of Solitude

On a beach with seagulls in a flurry,
I tossed my chips, oh what a hurry!
They squabbled and squawked like they owned the place,
I just giggled at their goofy face.

The tides keep rolling, they tease and they play,
I tried to surf, but I fell all day.
My friends all laughed, they couldn't take it,
I paddled back, 'Hey, let's don't fake it!'

The crabs on the sand, they dance with glee,
Waving their claws at the jellyfish spree.
I asked them to join in my beach day fun,
But they scuttled away, it's a crab's life, hon!

Shells clack together, a funky conch sound,
A conga line of fish, just having a round.
I tried to groove but tripped on a line,
The ocean laughs loud with its own sense of rhyme.

Silent Depths

Down below the waves, where fish wear suits,
I met a clam giving fashion disputes.
He said, "My pearl's got style, it's quite a sight!"
I laughed and said, "You glow in the night!"

A grouchy octopus juggled some rocks,
While a dolphin nearby performed with some socks.
They argued about who was the real sea king,
But it's hard to compete with an eel that can sing!

A shrimp with a hat served tea to a ray,
While turtles opted for a quiet ballet.
"Fancy a waltz?" the starfish asked with flair,
But I tripped on my fins and flew through the air!

The deep blue was rich with giggles and cheer,
When turtles came spinning, spreading their beer.
I tried to join in, but my twirls went astray,
And the fish all just burst into laughter that day.

Rhythm of the Seafoam

Seafoam dances like a frothy ballet,
Inviting the beachgoers who lay.
With sandcastles rising, a tower so tall,
A rogue wave giggles and gives it a fall.

The seagulls are gossiping, sharing their tales,
Of missing their flights and stolen fish scales.
I joined in the fun, asked for the scoop,
But they cawed in reply, "Join our beach troop!"

The sun beat down, but the shade was inviting,
A sunburned fellow was dramatically fighting.
His friends were all giggling—oh, what a scene!
He vowed to return, "Next time I'll be lean!"

The shells make a beat, what rhythm they spawn,
Crabs tap-dance, as day turns to dawn.
With laughter and bubbles, the waves take their cue,
In the comedy cast of the blue and the hue.

Blue Horizon's Lament

Oh, the horizon is calling, can't you hear?
With fishy tales, it brings us good cheer.
A whale with a hat sings the blues and more,
While flounders pretend to be fish on the floor.

The sun sets low, like a diva in peace,
While waves crash around, but the joy doesn't cease.
A crab in a sailor's cap gives a shout,
"Where's the punchline? Let's figure this out!"

The moon comes out, a spotlight on the scene,
As jellyfish glow like they're caught in a dream.
I yelled, "Make a wish!" as I tossed out a shell,
But a fish swam by and said, "Oh, what the hell!"

Each wave holds a story, each splash a new giggle,
With laughter and sprinkles of salted sea wiggle.
The blue horizon chuckles, it knows it can claim,
That life on its shores is a never-ending game.

Beneath the Ocean's Veil

Bubbles giggle near my ear,
A crab holds court, I lean and cheer.
The fish all laugh, they swim in style,
A seaweed dance, it makes me smile.

A dolphin's joke flies through the blue,
He tried to make a whale say moo!
The turtles nod, they think it's gold,
While jellyfish drift, both shy and bold.

A clownfish paints his face so bright,
Turns to a clown, he's quite the sight!
They prance around without a care,
All singing songs of salty air.

Underwater pranks make waves of cheer,
A shrimp-made band brings joy, oh dear!
So here I float, with smile so wide,
In this funny realm where fish abides.

The Depths of Conversation

In deep blue chats, the creatures meet,
A seahorse sways to a funky beat.
A sardine shares a tale so tall,
While octopus plays the mad maestro's call.

Starfish flip, they join the fun,
Debating who can shine the sun.
A clam joins in, but it's just a bleep,
With pearls of wisdom, he falls asleep.

The anglerfish tells a spooky tale,
Of how he once chased a tiny snail.
The others laugh and roll around,
For fishy gossip knows no bound.

Beneath the waves, the banter flows,
With splashes bright from fins and toes.
Their humor's fresh, like ocean spray,
In this underwater cabaret.

Tidal Secrets

Whispers ride on the foamy crest,
As crabs hold hands, they jest the best.
Anemones wave, in cheerful delight,
While sea cucumbers dance, oh what a sight!

A sea lion barks a wild old pun,
Waving his flippers, it's all in good fun.
The mackerels chuckle at silly things,
As a hermit crab juggles old ring bling.

In swirling tides, they play hide and seek,
The otters slip, and they all shriek.
With laughter bubbling, it's quite the spree,
In these tidal secrets, so wild and free!

The coral reefs hold their breaths and laugh,
As the gregarious group shares their silk-lined path.
For who needs silence when fish have a ball,
In the splashy realm where fun reigns for all!

Beneath the Waves

Beneath the waves, the giggles roll,
With every splash, there's humor's goal.
A pufferfish pops with a cheeky grin,
While flounders flop in a playful spin.

Octopi gossip with eight little arms,
Telling fish tales of sea bed charms.
The porpoises leap, in acrobatic cheer,
Soon joined by a school that swims quite near.

The sea urchins poke with jest so spry,
"Roll with us!" they tease, "Give it a try!"
But clams just laugh from their sandy beds,
As mullets weave through with big fish heads.

In the underwater dance-off, fins sway,
With laughter echoing through the spray.
So come take a dip in this whimsical space,
Where every wave has a smiling face.

Tides of Secrets

The waves conspire with the breeze,
Tickling shells beneath the trees.
Fish gossip, with fins a-flap,
While crabs dance in their secret tap.

Mermaids giggle with fishy friends,
Trading tales where the sea never ends.
Seaweed wigs on their heads so proud,
They laugh so hard, they attract a crowd.

The sand shifts, secrets unfold,
A beach ball juggles, or so I'm told.
But sneaky gulls have their own fun,
Stealing snacks while we all run.

So hold your laughter, don't let it drop,
The salty jesters just can't stop.
In ocean's laughter, we sail away,
Splashing joy in every wave.

Echoes Beneath the Waves

Bubbles bubbling with secrets spun,
Octopuses play peek-a-boo, oh what fun!
Starfish stare with their five set eyes,
Always surprised by their own disguise.

Crabs in their shells start a dance-off,
While sea cucumbers just scoff.
The barnacles grumble, stuck on a wall,
"Who needs freedom? We've got this crawl!"

Clams clap shells and join the jest,
Puff up proudly, they're the best dressed.
With sea slugs singing a silly tune,
It's a quirky party beneath the moon.

So dive on down for a giggle spree,
Where fish are chatty and wild and free.
In the depths, where laughter grows,
Follow the sound of jolly throes.

Salty Serenade

Seagulls squawk, with a jestful cheer,
As dolphins slide in the water near.
Jellyfish jiggle, their banners sway,
Floating along in a wobbly play.

Sandcastles crumble, all in good fun,
As the tide rolls in, it's a race to run.
A tidepool party with shrimp and more,
Dancing in shells, who could ask for more?

The surfboards flip in a splashing spree,
Surfers laughing, oh let it be!
But watch your toes, those starfish bite,
In this salty music, oh what a sight!

So tune your heart to the sea's own beat,
Let laughter rise, no need to retreat.
In this serenade of splashes and sighs,
Savor the joy, where the humor lies.

Murmurs of the Deep

Whales get chatty in a song so deep,
While squids perform and the lobsters leap.
Bubbles of laughter drift through the blue,
Professor Fish teaches, "Now here's what to do!"

Cranky clams call for a little respect,
While the flounders hide, making perfect suspect.
Sardines swim by in a shimmering rush,
Saying "Join the party! No need to hush!"

Pirate ghosts float with a wink and a cheer,
"Let's trade some treasure, if you dare come near!"
With anchored humor that drifts through the sea,
We're sailing on laughter, come share it with me!

So when you hear whispers from coral and sand,
Remember the joy that's waiting on hand.
In the depths where mirth grows lush and sweet,
Dive in for the giggles, oh isn't it neat?

Timeless Teal Tales

There once was a fish with a grin,
He wore a big hat, quite a win!
He danced in the waves, so carefree,
Said, 'I'm the prince of the sea, just wait and see!'

His friends tried to swim with some flair,
But flippers got tangled in the air.
They giggled and flopped, what a sight,
Splashing around from morning to night!

A crab joined the fun, dragging a drum,
His tiny legs grooved while others went thrum.
They formed a band with a splashy beat,
Music of bubbles echoed so sweet!

But then came a seagull with a squawk,
He stole their snacks, what a shock!
They laughed it away, such charm on the shore,
For laughter and snacks, they always want more!

Reflections on Blue

In the water, a dolphin took flight,
Wearing sunglasses, oh what a sight!
He slipped and he slid, chasing a ray,
Singing a tune, come join in the play!

A turtle strolled by with a sigh,
'You kids swim too fast, just let me lie!'
But the crew wouldn't stop for a break,
'Get up, Mr. Turtle, it's time to shake!'

Fish in a school tried to ballet,
But tangled their tails in a colorful fray.
Laughter erupted, the waves were alive,
In the dance of the sea, they began to thrive!

The starfish just shrugged, no hurry at all,
'Why rush for a world where we have a ball!'
With giggles and splashes, they twisted and twirled,
In their blue paradise, such joy was unfurled!

Oceanic Oracles

A wise old octopus, full of tales,
Wore robes of seaweed and quirky scales.
He said with a wink, 'Listen close, my friends,'
'Each wave brings a secret, a laugh that transcends!'

The guppies conspired, 'Let's find fortune!
We'll dig for pearls, chasing the current!'
But they stumbled on sand, tickling their toes,
Ended with giggles instead of gold shows!

A clam snapped shut, 'You're all quite mad,
Fortune's in laughter, and that's not so bad!'
They clacked and they cheered, their shells in delight,
Finding joy in the simple, oh what a night!

Starfish took notes on their silly plans,
She scribbled in sand, drawing happy clans.
With each ripple and splash, a memory grew,
In this quirky domain, the joy always flew!

Serenity in Sunrise

As dawn cracked, the waves looked so bright,
A seagull cracked jokes, oh what a sight!
He fueled up the sunrise with giggles and cheer,
Said, 'Don't mind the tides, grab a snack and steer!'

Crabs strutted proudly, sporting their shades,
Sassier than ever, they organized parades.
With little tambourines made of shells so neat,
They marched and they pranced, oh what a beat!

A whale joined the frolic, blowing bubbles galore,
'Who ordered a party? I'm ready for more!'
The surf sang along, a raucous refrain,
Together they danced through the soft, salty rain!

So as the sun rose, a jolly parade,
With laughter and splashing, no plans were betrayed.
In this buoyant world, joy flowed like the tide,
Emerging at sunrise, where secrets reside!

Horizon's Reflection

Waves crashing loudly, they tickle my toes,
Seagulls all laughing, they're stealing my nose.
Fish in their schools, they dance with such glee,
While I'm just flopping, a fish out of sea.

Shells whisper secrets, they giggle and play,
Mermaids on break, they sunbathe all day.
I try to catch crabs, but they run like the wind,
With a pinching pursuit, my laughter won't end.

Sandcastles crumble, my throne of pure dreams,
As waves plot against me, they burst at the seams.
Yet here in this chaos, smiles rise to the top,
In the splashy kingdom, we'll never stop!

So raise up your drink, let's toast to the sun,
Even when saltwater is stuck in my bun.
Each wave is a joke, each breeze has a pun,
Life by the shore is a barrel of fun!

Nature's Oceanic Echo

The water's a mirror, reflects every frown,
As crabs do the tango, they dance upside down.
Jellyfish jiggle, they float with such grace,
While I trip on the sand and fall flat on my face.

The tide brings in treasures, a sock or a shoe,
I hope it's a message, addressed just for you!
The dolphins are laughing, they flip for their meals,
While I'm here caught up, just watching their wheels.

Kites fly like fish, through the bright summer sky,
I try to catch wind but instead just say "Why?"
The sun casts its warmth, like butter on toast,
While I search for shade, but my hat is the ghost.

So join in this caper, let's frolic and glide,
The ocean's a character, full of laughter and pride.
With each wave that rolls in, there's fun to be found,
In the salty air, silliness abounds!

Beneath Starry Waters

Under the twinkle of stars shining bright,
Fish throw a party, a splashy delight.
They boogie and wiggle, a colorful crew,
While I ponder staying, lost in the blue.

Octopus paints pictures, with ink just for fun,
While whales sing ballads that make dolphins run.
I'm tangled in seaweed, my legs all a mess,
And the crabs all pass by, to admire my dress.

The sand tells a tale, of flip-flops gone wild,
As seahorses giggle, like some cheeky child.
The clams hold their jokes, behind rosy shells,
I laugh with the fish, as the laughter swells.

So here's to the nights, where the sea meets the shore,
With laughter and joy, always wanting some more.
In this underwater circus, let's dance and don't stop,
Life here is a project, let's hot air balloon hop!

Kisses from the Coast

The shoreline's a canvas, it changes with tides,
As seagulls roll in, like they're part of the rides.
I build little forts, made of shells and of sand,
Then knock them all down like they couldn't withstand.

Beach ball bounces high, but goes for a dive,
And the dog steals my sandwich, he's such a sly five!
With sun in my eyes, and a smile on my cheek,
The tide brings mischief, a wave full of squeak.

A crab tries to dance, like he's slick and suave,
While starfish just sit there, they don't even move.
The ocean's my buddy, though messy and wild,
Popcorn from waves makes me feel like a child.

So let's run down the sand, in a fast little race,
With laughter as our prize in this magical place.
The coast always kisses, with joy in the air,
As we splash 'round in water, without a single care!

www.ingramcontent.com/pod-product-compliance
Lightning Source LLC
Chambersburg PA
CBHW072135070526
44585CB00016B/1693